glycemic
Index
COOKBOOK

Delicious Low GI Recipes
lose weight • feel great • control blood sugar

Publications International, Ltd.

Pictured on the front cover: Grilled Chicken with Corn and Black Bean Salsa *(page 44)*.
Pictured on the back cover *(clockwise from top left):* Hoisin Beef Stir-Fry *(page 54)*, Tuna Tabbouleh Salad *(page 102)* and Chewy Mocha Brownie Cookies *(page 134)*.

ISBN-13: 978-1-60553-254-7
ISBN-10: 1-60553-254-1

Library of Congress Control Number: 2009940903

Manufactured in China.

8 7 6 5 4 3 2 1

Nutritional Analysis: Every effort has been made to check the accuracy of the nutritional information that appears with each recipe. However, because numerous variables account for a wide range of values for certain foods, nutritive analyses in this book should be considered approximate. Different results may be obtained by using different nutrient databases and different brand-name products.

Note: This book is for informational purposes and is not intended to provide medical advice. Neither Publications International, Ltd., nor the authors, editors or publisher takes responsibility for any possible consequences from any treatment, procedure, exercise, dietary modification, action, or applications of medication or preparation by any person reading or following the information in this cookbook. The publication of this book does not constitute the practice of medicine, and this cookbook does not replace your physician, pharmacist or health-care specialist. **Before undertaking any course of treatment or nutritional plan, the authors, editors and publisher advise the reader to check with a physician or other health-care provider.**

Publications International, Ltd.

contents

What Is the Glycemic Index?

Simply put, the glycemic index (GI for short) shows what happens to our blood sugar when we digest different types of carbohydrates. Carbohydrates that break down quickly raise blood sugar levels quickly and have a higher GI number. Those that take a longer time to digest turn into glucose more slowly and have a lower GI value.

Why Does It Matter?

The glycemic index was originally developed as a research tool for people with diabetes. Choosing carbohydrates with lower GI values could be part of a diet that helped manage blood sugar levels. But you don't need to be diabetic to know what a spike in blood sugar feels like. Most people have experienced a "sugar rush." You overeat sweet or starchy food and get a burst of energy, only to soon be followed by the need for a nap and the hunger for another candy bar. Avoiding these ups and downs makes it easier to maintain a healthy diet. Easily digested carbohydrates with high GI numbers can make you hungrier more quickly and more often. You'll probably also be more likely to reach for another quick sugar fix. This makes high GI foods a bad choice for those who want to watch their weight.

What Do All Those Numbers Mean?

The GI ranks foods according to their effect on blood sugar levels in comparison to a control food—glucose. Glucose is always assigned the number 100. The ranking is done by comparing the effect of 50 grams of carbohydrate in a particular food compared to 50 grams of glucose. The more a particular food raises blood sugar levels, the higher its GI number. Those that raise blood sugar less have a lower number.

Where Do the Numbers Come From?

There is a very strict testing protocol. Let's say researchers want to find out the GI value of a dried apricot. The subjects (usually 8 to 10 participants) are given enough dried apricots to provide 50 grams of available carbohydrate (approximately 27 apricot halves). Their blood sugar response is then tested and plotted on a graph every 15 minutes during the first hour and every 30 minutes during the second hour. The same procedure is used after they ingest 50 grams of glucose. The two values are compared and the data pulled from the graph is calculated.

In general, low GI foods have scores below 55. Moderate GI foods score 55 to 70, while high GI foods score above 70.

A Comparison of GI and GL Numbers

The following gives both the glycemic index and the glycemic load for some sample foods. Glycemic load is a better approximation of the effect on blood sugar of an actual serving of food. See page 6 for a full explanation of GL.

	GI	GL
Low GI (< 55)		
Low-fat yogurt with artificial sweetener	14	2
Lentils	28	5
Apple	36	6
All-Bran cereal	38	8
Tomato juice	38	4
Spaghetti	41	20
Canned baked beans	48	7
Orange, raw	48	5
Sourdough rye bread	48	6
100% stone ground whole-wheat bread	53	6
Sweet potato	54	17
Moderate (55–70)		
Brown rice	55	16
Oatmeal cookies	55	9
Moroccan couscous	58	23
Peach, canned in heavy syrup	58	9
Cheese pizza	60	16
Sweet corn	60	9
Split pea soup	60	16
Raisins	64	28
Grape Nuts cereal	67	15
Cranberry juice cocktail	68	24
Whole wheat bread	69	9
High (> 70)		
Toaster pastry	70	26
Skittles	70	32
Wonder, enriched white bread	71	10
Watermelon	72	4
Cheerios	74	15
Long-grain white rice, quick cooking	75	25
French fries	76	22
Russet potato, baked without fat	78	78
Jelly beans	80	22
Pretzels	83	19
French baguette	95	15

Going Beyond the Numbers

The glycemic index should not be used in isolation. We rarely eat a meal or snack that is ONLY a carbohydrate or a single food of any kind. The testing methods used to come up with the GI numbers can be misleading, too. Since food is being compared to 50 grams of glucose, which is pure carbohydrate, the test food must also contain 50 grams of carbohydrate. The tester may be consuming a lot more of something than you would in a normal serving size. This helps explain why some healthy foods have a surprisingly high GI number.

For example, watermelon has a GI of 72. Knowing that might lead you to avoid watermelon, even though it's a healthy food and a great source of phytochemicals such as lycopene. What the GI doesn't tell you is that it takes more than 4½ cups of watermelon to provide the 50 grams of available carbohydrate on which GI is calculated. That's nine times the amount in a typical ½ cup serving!

Or, consider the dried apricot example on page 5. To perform the test, participants had to consume 27 apricot halves. That's a lot of fruit!

Fortunately there's another helpful number—glycemic load—that makes it easier to judge an actual serving of a food.

Glycemic Load: What It Means and How to Use It

The glycemic load number (GL for short) gives you a truer picture of what effect a typical serving of a food will have on blood sugar. It is calculated by multiplying the amount of available carbohydrate in a typical serving of food by the GI number and then dividing the result by 100.

For example, a typical serving of watermelon is ½ cup, the amount of available carbohydrate in it is 5.75 grams, and its GI is 72. Here's how the GL is calculated: 5.75 X 72 divided by 100. The result is 4.14, which is rounded to get its glycemic load rating of 4. Watermelon doesn't seem like a high GI food anymore, does it? Most GI charts also include GL numbers, so there's no need to do the math yourself!

Nobody Eats Just a Potato

Many other factors influence human digestion and the release of glucose into the bloodstream. For instance, if you eat protein or fat along with a carbohydrate, it is digested more slowly. Potato chips actually have a lower GI than a baked potato because they contain fat, but that doesn't mean they're a better food choice! Here are some other factors that influence glycemic values.

• **Degree of ripeness**

For example, the more ripe a banana is, the higher its GI. This typically applies to all fruits that continue to ripen once harvested.

• **Presence of acid**

Acid slows the rate at which your body digests a particular food. Slower digestion means slower absorption and a more favorable effect on blood sugar.

• **Individual differences**

Test five people and each will respond differently to the same food. That's why GI numbers are sometimes revised as more tests are done.

• **Type of flour**

Finely milled flours have high GI values. Stone-ground flours and grainy breads take longer to digest.

• **Cooking time**

Cooking makes starch molecules swell and softens them. Al dente pasta has a lower GI than pasta that is overcooked.

• **Other ingredients**

If a high GI carbohydrate is combined with, or eaten with, food containing fat or protein, digestion is slowed and blood sugar response moderated.

Is GI Just Another Low-Carb Diet?

The glycemic index only provides values for carbohydrates. Foods made of only fat or protein always have a GI number of zero. But a low GI diet is not the same as a low-carb diet. It's a good carb diet. With low GI you replace refined, starchy, sugary carbs with good carbs, such as beans and vegetables. Anyone who has been on an extremely low-carb diet knows that although the regimen may help you lose weight short term, it is not a sustainable plan. Low GI eating is a lifestyle change, not a short-term crash diet.

Why Carbohydrates Are So Important

The primary function of all carbohydrates is to provide energy, particularly for the brain and nervous system. Plants are rich in carbohydrates, as that is their storage form of energy. When we eat plant-based foods, we put this stored energy to use within the body. Although we can use protein and fat to produce energy, carbohydrates are the body's preferred fuel since they are quickest and easiest to metabolize.

Metabolism 101

We don't eat continuously, but our bodies need glucose all the time to keep running. Glucose molecules are absorbed and used by trillions of cells throughout the body. A delicate regulatory system maintains tight control over the level of glucose in the blood. When you eat a carbohydrate-containing food, your digestive tract breaks it down into simple glucose molecules and blood sugar levels rise. Insulin, a hormone released from your pancreas, helps glucose enter your cells, where it is used to produce energy. What can't be used is stored in the form of fat. This is an oversimplification, but it gives you an idea of the process.

So if all carbs turn into glucose, why does it matter which ones you eat? High GI, refined carbs are practically predigested. It takes very little time to break the chemical bonds and send a surge of glucose roaring into the blood. Insulin tries to keep up, but more glucose can end up stored as fat. A rush of energy occurs, but in a few hours it's gone and hunger recurs. This sounds like a recipe for weight gain because it is.

Replacing Refined Carbs with Good Carbs

The glycemic index can help you tell the good guys from the bad guys. There are also some general guidelines. Refined carbs tend to be pale and wan. Think of refined white bread, white rice and potatoes. This doesn't mean you can never enjoy any of these foods again, just that you should cut back significantly on portion sizes and replace them with good carbs wherever possible.

Swapping High GI for Low GI

Instead of:	Choose:
Cold cereal	Oatmeal (not instant)
Orange juice	Orange
White bread	Stone-ground whole wheat Bread
White rice	Lentils or barley
Potatoes	Beans
French fries	Veggies and dip
Soda	Sparkling water
Cake	Fresh fruit

Does Fat Make You Fat?

It sounds convincing—and certainly companies selling fat-free foods would like you to believe—that removing fat is the key to losing weight. Unfortunately, fat-free is far from calorie-free. In fact, to make fat-free goods palatable, fat is usually replaced with sugar or other refined carbohydrates. The other problem is that fat keeps your hunger satisfied longer. No wonder the fat-free craze didn't do much to trim our waistlines!

The Kind of Fat Matters

Fats and oils moderate the speed of absorption of high GI foods. They also make things taste good. But before you start piling on the butter, you need to consider some other information. There is convincing evidence that saturated fat may raise cholesterol. Just as with carbohydrate, the kind of fat you eat matters.

Saturated Versus Unsaturated Fat

Unsaturated fats are derived from plant sources and saturated fats come mainly from animal products. These terms refer to whether all the chemical bonds between carbon and hydrogen atoms are all filled or "saturated." Never mind that—there's an easy way to tell. Saturated

fats are solid at room temperature. Good fats, the unsaturated ones, are liquid. If you've heard of the benefits of the Mediterranean diet, it won't surprise you to learn that olive oil is believed by many nutritionists to actually be beneficial for the heart and blood vessels.

Fat and the GI Diet

The good news is that if you are eating more fruits and vegetables and less processed food, you are probably cutting way down on fat without even trying. Don't hesitate to cook with a few tablespoons of olive oil or add a pat of butter to your broccoli. The worst fats, such as trans fats, are usually used to make high GI starchy carbs taste good or have a longer shelf life. Think deep-fried restaurant fare or packaged cookies and cakes.

Substituting Good Fats for Bad Fats

1. Cook with olive oil. If you need flavorless oil, try canola or grapeseed oil. If the recipe requires the rich taste of butter, you can usually replace half of it with oil without compromising flavor.

2. Change your dressing. Store-bought salad dressings can be loaded with sugar or preservatives. Make a simple vinaigrette with olive oil, or just pass a good quality vinegar and olive oil at the table.

3. Avoid processed meat. It can hide bad fat and sometimes bad carbs, too.

4. Choose low-fat dairy. Drink low-fat milk. Watch out for cheese. It can contribute a lot of fat to food, most of it saturated. Try using small amounts of full-flavored cheeses like Parmesan.

5. Cook at home. Deep-fried chicken, potatoes and fish from restaurants are very likely to contain high levels of trans fats. Home-cooked meals are almost always healthier.

6. Go fish. Fatty fish, such as salmon, tuna and sardines, contain beneficial omega-3 fatty acids. These fats appear to improve cholesterol.

Some Whole Grain History

Long before processed foods, 24-hour convenience marts and supermarkets that carry thousands of foods under one roof, humans ate foods in their natural, whole state. Fruits, vegetables, nuts and seeds were a significant part of the human diet. We ate what nature provided, the way nature provided it.

My, how things have changed! One of the biggest transformations was the introduction of mills to grind grain. First came stones that produced a coarse product. Then steel rollers arrived that could finely mill vast fields of grain quickly. We also learned how to refine wheat flour even further into white flour. This gave bread and other baked goods more visual and textural appeal. Every step of the way, these processes removed the healthy bran and germ of wheat and raised its glycemic index.

Grains of Sense

What exactly are whole grains? They are the entire edible portion of any grain, including corn, wheat, rice and others. Refining removes the bran (outer shell) and the germ (embryo) of the grain. White flour and cornmeal are two examples of highly refined grains in many foods we eat. Unfortunately, a lot of fiber, vitamins and antioxidants are discarded with the germ and bran.

Choosing whole grain products isn't as easy as buying the brown loaf of bread instead of the white one. Even when a label says multigrain, what's inside may be made from refined flour. Check the ingredients label. If the first ingredient is whole wheat flour or another whole grain flour, then you're getting what you want. If it just says wheat flour, you're getting refined flour, and that deep brown color may have come from added caramel coloring.

The Fiber Factor

Fiber in a carbohydrate slows down the absorption of glucose into the bloodstream. You feel fuller longer. There are plenty of other benefits to fiber. Fiber found in oats, barley and most fruits and vegetables helps remove LDL cholesterol from the body. Fiber found in lentils, beans and other legumes can help you maintain regularity and prevent many gastrointestinal problems. The recommended amount for daily fiber is 20 to 35 grams and most of us don't get nearly enough. Changing to a low GI diet can help. You'll be adding fiber with every serving of vegetables, fruits, beans and lentils.

Do you eat enough fiber (20–35 grams) in a day?

Write in the number of daily servings you eat for each food type*:	Multiply by the fiber (in grams)	Total Your Day's Fiber Intake (in grams)
Beans, lentils ____ servings	X 6	_____
Fruits, vegetables, whole grain products, nuts ____ servings	X 2.5	_____
Refined grain products ____ servings (white bread, white rice, regular pasta)	X 1	_____
Other grain products (including cereal) *(Check the label for the number of grams)*	X _____	_____
Total daily grams of dietary fiber		_____

*Daily serving sizes
- beans, lentils = ½ cup
- fruit = ½ cup canned or frozen, 1 medium size whole fruit, ½ cup juice
- vegetables = 1 cup raw, leafy vegetables, ½ cup cooked vegetables
- whole grain products = 1 slice bread, 1 cup dry cereal, ½ cup cooked pasta or rice
- nuts = 1 ounce

Fiber—going, going, gone

What happens to healthy, nutrient-packed carbohydrate foods that end up overprocessed and shipped out to grocers' shelves? Here's an example:

Apple, medium, raw with skin	80 calories	3.7 grams of fiber
Applesauce, ½ cup, sweetened	97 calories	1.5 grams of fiber
Apple juice, from frozen concentrate, ½ cup	84 calories	0 grams of fiber
Corn, ½ cup, frozen	66 calories	2.0 grams of fiber
Corn flakes, 1 cup	102 calories	1.1 grams of fiber
Corn syrup, 1 tablespoon	60 calories	0 grams of fiber

Indulge in Delicious

Low GI eating is not about depriving yourself. It's about enjoying more fruits, vegetables and whole grains every day. The recipes in this book will get you started on the right track.

Get inspired to try something new and different at least once a week. Variety makes healthy eating a delicious adventure instead of an exercise in self control.

Beans & Lentils: Stars of the Glycemic Index

There may not be an easier, better, tastier way to add low GI nutrition to your meals than eating beans more frequently. Beans, lentils and chickpeas provide protein, fiber, B vitamins and minerals. They are inexpensive and convenient, especially in cans. (Higher sodium levels in canned beans can be somewhat lowered by rinsing beans before cooking.) They come in a kaleidoscope of colors and shapes and are an important part of most every cuisine. From Asia's soybeans to Italy's cannellini beans to Mexico's pintos, beans offer many delectable options.

Black
(turtle bean, frijoles negros)
Black beans are a staple in Latin American dishes. Their strong, earthy flavor and firm texture help them stand out in soups, salads and all sorts of side dishes.

Cannellini (white kidney bean)
Mild-tasting, meaty cannellinis are often used in minestrone soup and other Italian dishes.

Chickpea (garbanzo bean)
The versatile chickpea has a rich, buttery flavor and is a nutritional powerhouse with over 80 nutrients, plus plenty of fiber and protein.

Cranberry
(shell bean, Roman, borlotti)
This pretty oval-shaped bean is streaked with red, both inside and out. The flavor is often described as earthy or nutty. Cranberry beans are also available as fresh shell beans during the summer.

Great Northern
This large, mild white bean is a favorite in casseroles, stews and soups. Great Northerns are also commonly used in baked beans and bean dips.

Lentils

Lentils cook quickly and are often served puréed. The most common varieties are brown and red, but for a larger selection explore the many different kinds used in Indian and Middle Eastern cuisines.

Lima (butter)

If you think you don't like limas but you've only had canned, give them another chance. Their rich, buttery flavor holds up better when they're frozen or fresh.

Navy
(Boston, Yankee, pea bean)

The name comes from the fact that they've been served in the Navy since 1800. These small white beans are used to make canned pork and beans, but they are good in chili and soups as well.

Pinto

Speckled beige beans with darker streaks, pintos are used for refried beans, chili and many Mexican recipes. Unfortunately, their distinctive markings turn a dull pinkish-beige after cooking.

Red kidney

Kidney beans are full flavored and retain their kidney shape even with long cooking times. They are usually the bean of choice for chili or cold salads.

Soybean (edamame)

Soybeans are an economical source of protein, providing all of the amino acids typically found in animal products without the saturated fat and cholesterol. They are readily available frozen, shelled or in the pod, and make a great snack.

Beyond Wheat

Eating low GI is a wonderful excuse to try some less familiar grains. Check the bulk bins at the market and start by trying a small amount of something you're unsure of. Here are some low GI options.

Barley

Barley is one of the oldest cereal grains and has the lowest GI value of just about any of them. Don't limit it to soup—try a barley pilaf or stew.

Basmati rice

Although rice is a whole grain, many kinds have a high GI. This has to do with how much the starch expands during cooking. Basmati, which is a fragrant, long grain variety popular in India, has a lower GI because it cooks up dry and fluffy.

Buckwheat

Strictly speaking, buckwheat is an herb, not a grain. The seeds of the plant have been ground and made into noodles and baked goods for centuries. Kasha is the name for toasted buckwheat groats.

Bulgur

Bulgur is a form of wheat used in many Middle Eastern and Mediterranean dishes. It's quick cooking and delicious in tabbouleh, pilafs and mixed into meatballs or meat loaf.

Quinoa

Try this protein-packed grain that cooks up quickly and tastes light and delicate. Use it hot or cold, in salads or side dishes.

Tips for Adding Veggies to Your Diet

1. Make it easy on yourself. Choose prewashed bags of vegetables or bring home goodies from the salad bar at your local supermarket.

2. Fight snack attacks. Instead of grabbing cookies or a soda, keep baby carrots, celery sticks, cherry tomatoes or sugar snap peas on hand for snacking.

3. Go vegetarian once a week. Plan a whole meal around a vegetable-based main dish. Try a stir-fry, soup or pasta creation.

4. Add veggies to favorites. Order a pizza with vegetable topping or add veggies to a frozen pie. Shred carrots or zucchini into meat loaf or muffins. Grill bell peppers and zucchini alongside burgers or steak.

5. Try something new and different. Add color and flavor to your menus with less mainstream vegetables. Try Asian eggplant, kale or different varieties of more common veggies, such as Italian-style green beans.

6. Grow your own or shop locally. Grow vegetables in your garden or visit a farmers' market or produce stand. In-season fresh vegetables are so delicious they make it easy to get your vitamins.

It's a Way of Life, Not a Short-Term Diet!

Controlling your weight and your blood sugar is not a short-term project. The glycemic index can help you understand better ways to eat a healthier diet, but it is not a quick fix or a magic bullet. Adding more vegetables and fruit to what you eat every day and cutting back on refined carbohydrates and starches needs to be a permanent lifestyle change. Fortunately, it is one that can be truly enjoyable and that becomes second nature over time. Once you start choosing carbohydrates that have low glycemic loads instead of high ones, it's easier to control your cravings. With the recipes in this book, you're off to a great start.

The Glycemic Index FAQ

1. What is glucose? It is the simplest, most essential sugar molecule and the source of energy for all the body's cells.

2. What is blood sugar? The glucose that is traveling in your bloodstream at any given time is called blood sugar.

3. What is a glycemic response? The measure of a particular food's ability to raise blood sugar is called a glycemic response. The glycemic index is based on the amount of elevation.

4. Where can I find a complete listing of GI numbers? There are many websites offering the glycemic index numbers for a variety of foods. Because research is ongoing, new foods are constantly added.

5. Why doesn't every food have a GI number? Only carbohydrates can be tested by this methodology, not fat or protein.

6. What foods are forbidden on the GI Diet? None. Even foods with a high GI number can have a place in a healthy diet. The GI is a tool to help you make better choices.

7. Is glycemic load (GL) the same as glycemic index (GI)? The glycemic load of a food is derived from its GI number based on a mathematical formula. (See page 6 for details.) It is a better approximation of the effect an actual serving size of food will have on blood sugar.

8. Why do some healthy foods (baked potatoes) have higher GIs than unhealthy versions (potato chips and French fries)? The fat in foods slows down the rate of digestion and so makes the GI lower. Don't be fooled! Saturated fat is still unhealthy and the excess calories it carries make a difference.

goat cheese & tomato omelet

    3 egg whites
    2 eggs
    1 tablespoon water
    ⅛ teaspoon salt
    ⅛ teaspoon black pepper
        Nonstick cooking spray
    ⅓ cup crumbled goat cheese
    1 plum tomato, diced (⅓ cup)
    2 tablespoons chopped fresh basil or parsley

1. Whisk together egg whites, eggs, water, salt and pepper in medium bowl.

2. Spray medium nonstick skillet with cooking spray; place over medium heat. Add egg mixture; cook 2 minutes or until eggs begin to set on bottom. Gently lift edge of omelet to allow uncooked portion of eggs to flow to underneath. Cook 3 minutes or until center is almost set.

3. Sprinkle cheese, tomato and basil over half of omelet. Fold omelet over filling. Continue cooking 1 to 2 minutes or until cheese begins to melt and center is set. Cut omelet in half; transfer to serving plates.

Makes 2 servings

Nutrients per Serving: Calories: 80, Carbohydrate: 2g, Total Fat: 5g, Saturated Fat: 3g, Fiber: 0g

sweet potato pancakes with apple-cherry chutney

Apple-Cherry Chutney (recipe follows)
1 pound sweet potatoes (about 2 medium), peeled
½ small onion
3 egg whites
2 tablespoons all-purpose flour
½ teaspoon salt
¼ teaspoon black pepper
4 teaspoons vegetable oil, divided

1. Prepare Apple-Cherry Chutney; set aside.

2. Cut potatoes into chunks. Combine potatoes, onion, egg whites, flour, salt and pepper in food processor or blender; process until almost smooth (mixture will appear grainy).

3. Heat large nonstick skillet over medium heat 1 minute. Add 1 teaspoon oil. Spoon ⅓ cup batter per pancake into skillet. Cook 3 pancakes at a time, 3 minutes per side or until golden brown. Repeat with remaining oil and batter. Serve with Apple-Cherry Chutney. **Makes 6 servings**

apple-cherry chutney: Combine 1 cup chunky applesauce, ½ cup tart cherries, 2 tablespoons brown sugar, 1 teaspoon lemon juice, ½ teaspoon cinnamon and ⅛ teaspoon nutmeg in small saucepan. Bring to a boil. Reduce heat; simmer 5 minutes. Serve warm.

Nutrients per Serving: Calories: 139, Carbohydrate: 25g, Total Fat: 3g, Saturated Fat: <1g, Fiber: 3g

confetti scones

2 teaspoons olive oil

⅓ cup minced red bell pepper

⅓ cup minced green bell pepper

½ teaspoon dried thyme

1 cup all-purpose flour

¼ cup whole wheat flour

1½ teaspoons baking powder

½ teaspoon baking soda

½ teaspoon sugar

¼ teaspoon ground red pepper

⅛ teaspoon salt

⅓ cup sour cream

⅓ cup fat-free skim milk

2 tablespoons minced green onions

¼ cup grated Parmesan cheese

1. Preheat oven to 400°F. Line baking sheet with parchment paper.

2. Heat oil in small skillet over medium heat. Add bell peppers and thyme; cook and stir 5 minutes or until tender. Combine flours, baking powder, baking soda, sugar, ground red pepper and salt in large bowl. Add sour cream, milk, green onions and bell pepper mixture; mix to form sticky dough. Stir in cheese. *(Do not overmix.)*

3. Drop dough by rounded tablespoonfuls onto prepared baking sheet. Place in oven and immediately reduce heat to 375°F. Bake 13 to 15 minutes or until golden. Remove to wire rack; cool completely.

Makes 24 scones

Nutrients per Serving: Calories: 37, Carbohydrate: 6g, Total Fat: 1g, Saturated Fat: <1g, Fiber: <1g

very berry yogurt parfaits

    3 cups plain fat-free yogurt
    2 tablespoons sugar-free berry preserves
    1 packet sugar substitute*
    ½ teaspoon vanilla
    2 cups sliced fresh strawberries
    1 cup fresh blueberries
    4 tablespoons sliced toasted almonds

This recipe was tested with sucralose-based sugar substitute.

1. Combine yogurt, preserves, sugar substitute and vanilla in medium bowl.

2. Layer ½ cup yogurt mixture, ¼ cup strawberries, ¼ cup blueberries and ¼ cup yogurt mixture in each of 4 dessert dishes. Top each parfait with remaining ¼ cup strawberries and 1 tablespoon almonds. Serve immediately.   **Makes 4 servings**

note: These parfaits would also be delicious topped with low-fat granola. Or, try another flavor of preserves for a simple variation.

Nutrients per Serving: Calories: 179, Carbohydrate: 33g, Total Fat: 3g, Saturated Fat: <1g, Fiber: 3g

TIP

Start the day with a low GI breakfast instead of a sugary muffin or cereal and you'll feel satisfied longer. Think outside the usual choices and try fruit, yogurt, old-fashioned oats or a veggie omelet. There's evidence that eating a healthy breakfast aids everything from energy levels to weight loss. Chances are you'll like the difference in how you feel for the rest of the day.

fruited granola

3 cups old-fashioned oats

1 cup sliced almonds

1 cup honey

½ cup wheat germ or honey wheat germ

3 tablespoons butter or margarine, melted

1 teaspoon ground cinnamon

3 cups whole-grain cereal flakes

½ cup dried blueberries or golden raisins

½ cup dried cranberries or cherries

½ cup dried banana chips or chopped pitted dates

1. Preheat oven to 325°F.

2. Spread oats and almonds in single layer in 13×9-inch baking pan. Bake 15 minutes or until lightly toasted, stirring frequently.

3. Combine honey, wheat germ, butter and cinnamon in large bowl until well blended. Add oats and almonds; toss to coat completely. Spread mixture in single layer in baking pan. Bake 20 minutes or until golden brown. Cool completely in pan on wire rack. Break mixture into chunks.

4. Combine oat chunks, cereal, blueberries, cranberries and banana chips in large bowl. Store in airtight container at room temperature up to 2 weeks. Makes about 20 (½-cup) servings

Nutrients per Serving: Calories: 210, Carbohydrate: 36g, Total Fat: 7g, Saturated Fat: 2g, Fiber: 4g

TIP ———————————o o o—
Prepare this granola on the weekend and you'll have a scrumptious snack or breakfast treat on hand for the rest of the week!

veggie-beef hash

4 ounces cooked roast beef, finely chopped

1 1/2 cups frozen seasoning blend*

1 cup shredded potatoes

1/2 cup shredded carrots

1 egg white or 2 tablespoons liquid egg white

1/2 teaspoon dried rosemary

1/2 teaspoon black pepper

Nonstick cooking spray

1/2 cup salsa (optional)

Frozen seasoning blend is a combination of finely chopped onion, celery, green and red bell peppers and parsley flakes. Frozen or fresh sliced bell peppers and onion can be substituted.

1. Combine beef, seasoning blend, potatoes, carrots, egg white, rosemary and black pepper in large bowl.

2. Lightly spray large nonstick skillet with cooking spray; heat over medium-high heat. Add beef mixture; press down firmly to form large cake. Cook 4 minutes or until browned on bottom, pressing down on cake several times. Turn. Cook 4 minutes or until lightly browned and heated through. Serve with salsa, if desired.   Makes 2 servings

Nutrients per Serving: Calories: 297, Carbohydrate: 33g, Total Fat: 9g, Saturated Fat: 2g, Fiber: 5g

california omelet with avocado

6 ounces plum tomato, chopped (about 1½ tomatoes)
2 to 4 tablespoons chopped cilantro
¼ teaspoon salt
2 cups cholesterol-free egg substitute
¼ cup fat-free (skim) milk
Nonstick cooking spray
1 ripe medium avocado, chopped
1 small cucumber, chopped
1 lemon, quartered

1. Preheat oven to 200°F. Combine tomatoes, cilantro and salt in small bowl; set aside.

2. Whisk egg substitute and milk in medium bowl until well blended.

3. Heat small nonstick ovenproof skillet over medium heat; coat with cooking spray. Pour half of egg mixture into skillet; cook 2 minutes or until eggs begin to set. Lift edge of omelet to allow uncooked portion to flow underneath. Cook 3 minutes or until set.

4. Spoon half of tomato mixture over half of omelet. Loosen omelet with spatula and fold in half. Slide omelet onto serving plate; keep warm. Repeat steps for second omelet with remaining half of egg mixture. Serve topped with avocado and cucumber and garnish with lemon wedges.

Makes 4 servings

Nutrients per Serving: Calories: 145, Carbohydrate: 13g, Total Fat: 5g, Saturated Fat: 1g, Fiber: 4g

smoked sausage & red pepper frittata

  Nonstick cooking spray
7 ounces smoked turkey sausage, diced
1 medium red bell pepper, diced
1 medium yellow squash, sliced
½ cup finely chopped yellow onion
1 cup cholesterol-free egg substitute
1 package (3 ounces) reduced-fat cream cheese
  Salt and black pepper
¼ cup fresh salsa

1. Lightly coat large nonstick skillet with nonstick cooking spray. Add sausage. Cook over high heat 2 to 3 minutes or until beginning to brown, stirring frequently. Set aside on plate.

2. Coat same skillet with nonstick cooking spray; reduce heat to medium-high. Add bell pepper, squash and onion. Coat vegetables with cooking spray. Cook and stir 4 minutes or until onions are translucent.

3. Meanwhile, place egg substitute, cream cheese and black pepper in blender. Purée until smooth.

4. Reduce heat to medium-low; stir in sausage. Pour egg substitute mixture evenly over all. Cover; cook 10 minutes or until almost set. Remove from heat, let stand uncovered 3 to 4 minutes. Cut into quarters. Top each serving with 1 tablespoon salsa.   **Makes 4 servings**

note: This frittata is delicious served at room temperature as well.

Nutrients per Serving: Calories: 170, Carbohydrate: 13g, Total Fat: 5g, Saturated Fat: 3g, Fiber: 2g

mixed berry whole grain coffee cake

1 ¼ cups all-purpose flour, divided
¾ cup old-fashioned oats
¾ cup packed light brown sugar
3 tablespoons butter, softened
1 cup whole wheat flour
1 cup fat-free (skim) milk
¾ cup granulated sugar
¼ cup canola oil
1 egg, slightly beaten
1 tablespoon baking powder
1 teaspoon ground cinnamon
½ teaspoon salt
1 ½ cups frozen unsweetened mixed berries, thawed and drained
      or 2 cups fresh berries
¼ cup chopped walnuts

1. Preheat oven to 350°F. Coat 9×5×3-inch loaf pan with nonstick cooking spray; set aside.

2. Combine ¼ cup all-purpose flour, oats, brown sugar and butter in small bowl. Mix with fork until crumbly; set aside.

3. Combine remaining 1 cup all-purpose flour, whole wheat flour, milk, granulated sugar, oil, egg, baking powder, cinnamon and salt in large bowl. Beat with electric mixer or whisk 1 to 2 minutes until well blended. Fold in berries.

4. Spread batter in prepared pan. Sprinkle evenly with reserved oat mixture. Top with chopped walnuts. Bake 38 to 40 minutes or until toothpick inserted into center comes out clean. Serve warm.

Makes 12 servings

Nutrients per Serving: Calories: 272, Carbohydrate: 42g, Total Fat: 10g, Saturated Fat: 3g, Fiber: 3g

breakfast oats

> 1 ½ cups old-fashioned oats
> 3 cups water
> 2 cups chopped peeled apples
> ¼ cup sliced almonds
> ½ teaspoon ground cinnamon

slow cooker directions

Combine oats, water, apples, almonds and cinnamon in slow cooker.
Cover; cook on LOW 8 hours.   **Makes 6 (½-cup) servings**

Nutrients per Serving: Calories: 119, Carbohydrate: 20g, Total Fat: 3g,
Saturated Fat: <1g, Fiber: 4g

creamy oatmeal

> 1 ⅓ cups old-fashioned oats
> 3 cups fat-free (skim) milk
> ½ cup raisins
> 4 teaspoons sugar
> ⅛ teaspoon salt

1. Combine oats, milk, raisins, sugar and salt in medium saucepan over
medium heat.

2. Bring to a boil, stirring occasionally. Reduce heat and simmer 5 minutes.
Cover; remove from heat. Let stand 5 minutes.

Makes 6 (¾-cup) servings

tip: For a quick, make-ahead breakfast, freeze oatmeal in individual
portions. It can be reheated quickly in the microwave.

Nutrients per Serving: Calories: 159, Carbohydrate: 31g, Total Fat: 1g,
Saturated Fat: <1g, Fiber: 2g

main course makeover

●○○

greek-style salmon

- 1½ teaspoons olive oil
- 1¾ cups diced tomatoes, drained
- 6 black olives, coarsely chopped
- 4 green olives, coarsely chopped
- 3 tablespoons lemon juice
- 2 tablespoons chopped fresh Italian parsley
- 1 tablespoon capers, rinsed and drained
- 2 cloves garlic, thinly sliced
- ¼ teaspoon black pepper
- 1 pound salmon fillets

1. Heat oil in large skillet over medium-high heat. Add tomatoes, olives, lemon juice, parsley, capers, garlic and pepper; bring to a simmer over medium heat, stirring frequently.

2. Simmer tomato mixture 5 minutes or until reduced by about one third, stirring occasionally.

3. Rinse salmon and pat dry with paper towels. Push sauce to one side of skillet. Add salmon to skillet; spoon sauce over salmon. Cover and cook 10 to 15 minutes or until salmon begins to flake when tested with fork.

Makes 4 servings

Nutrients per Serving: Calories: 254, Carbohydrate: 6g, Total Fat: 15g, Saturated Fat: 3g, Fiber: 2g

steak diane with cremini mushrooms

Nonstick cooking spray

2 beef tenderloin steaks (4 ounces each), cut ¾ inch thick

Salt and black pepper

⅓ cup sliced shallots or chopped onion

4 ounces cremini mushrooms, sliced or 1 (4-ounce) package sliced mixed wild mushrooms

1½ tablespoons Worcestershire sauce

1 tablespoon Dijon mustard

1. Spray large nonstick skillet with nonstick cooking spray; heat over medium-high heat. Add steaks; season with salt and pepper. Cook 3 minutes per side for medium-rare or to desired doneness. Transfer to plate; cover to keep warm.

2. Spray same skillet with cooking spray; place over medium heat. Add shallots; cook and stir 2 minutes. Add mushrooms; cook 3 minutes, stirring frequently. Add Worcestershire sauce and mustard; cook 1 minute, stirring frequently.

3. Return steaks and any accumulated juices to skillet; heat through, turning once. Transfer steaks to serving plates; top with mushroom mixture.

Makes 2 servings

Nutrients per Serving: Calories: 239, Carbohydrate: 10g, Total Fat: 9g, Saturated Fat: 3g, Fiber: 1g

thai basil pork stir-fry

1 pound pork tenderloin, sliced across the grain into ¼-inch slices

1 tablespoon light soy sauce

½ teaspoon minced garlic

2 tablespoons canola oil

1 bag (16 ounces) ready-to-use fresh broccoli florets

1 medium red bell pepper, cut into strips

1 to 2 tablespoons Thai green curry paste*

1¼ cups chicken broth

2 tablespoons chopped fresh basil

2 tablespoons finely chopped roasted peanuts

3 cups fresh mung bean sprouts

*Thai green curry paste is available in the ethnic section of most supermarkets in cans or jars. Use 1 tablespoon for a mildly spicy dish or 2 tablespoons for a hot dish.

1. Combine pork, soy sauce and garlic in medium bowl; toss to coat.

2. Heat oil in large nonstick skillet over high heat. Add broccoli; stir-fry 3 to 4 minutes or until broccoli begins to brown. Add bell pepper; stir-fry 1 minute. Add pork mixture and curry paste; stir-fry 2 minutes. Add broth; cook and stir 2 to 3 minutes or until heated through.

3. Remove from heat; stir in chopped basil.

4. Serve with bean sprouts and sprinkle with peanuts.

Makes 6 servings

Nutrients per Serving: Calories: 199, Carbohydrate: 9g, Total Fat: 8g, Saturated Fat: 1g, Fiber: 3g

grilled chicken with corn & black bean salsa

½ cup corn

½ can black beans, rinsed and drained

½ cup finely chopped red bell pepper

½ ripe medium avocado, diced

1 jalapeño pepper,* minced

¼ cup chopped cilantro

2 tablespoons lime juice

½ teaspoon salt, divided

1 teaspoon black pepper

½ teaspoon chili powder

4 boneless skinless chicken breasts (4 ounces each), pounded to ½-inch thickness

Nonstick cooking spray

*Jalapeño peppers can sting and irritate the skin, so wear rubber gloves when handling peppers and do not touch your eyes.

1. Combine corn, black beans, bell pepper, avocado, jalapeños, cilantro, lime juice and ¼ teaspoon salt in medium bowl.

2. Combine black pepper, chili powder and remaining ¼ teaspoon salt in small bowl; sprinkle over chicken.

3. Coat grill pan with cooking spray and heat over medium-high heat. Cook chicken 4 minutes per side or until no longer pink in center.

4. Serve each chicken breast with ¼ cup salsa. Refrigerate remaining salsa for another use. Makes 4 servings

Nutrients per Serving: Calories: 230, Carbohydrate: 16g, Total Fat: 7g, Saturated Fat: 1g, Fiber: 5g

layered taco salad

Nonstick cooking spray

½ pound 95% lean ground beef

1½ teaspoons chili powder

1½ teaspoons ground cumin, divided

½ cup picante sauce

1 teaspoon sugar

6 cups shredded romaine lettuce

2 plum tomatoes, seeded and diced

½ cup chopped green onions

¼ cup chopped fresh cilantro

28 nacho-flavored baked tortilla chips, crumbled (2 ounces)

½ cup fat-free sour cream

½ cup (2 ounces) shredded reduced-fat sharp Cheddar or Mexican blend cheese

1. Spray medium nonstick skillet with cooking spray; heat over medium-high heat. Brown beef 3 to 5 minutes, stirring to break up meat. Drain fat. Stir in chili powder and 1 teaspoon cumin. Let cool.

2. Combine picante sauce, sugar and remaining ½ teaspoon cumin in small bowl.

3. Place lettuce in 11×7-inch casserole dish. Layer with beef, tomatoes, green onions, cilantro and chips. Top with sour cream; sprinkle with cheese. Spoon picante sauce mixture on top.

Makes 4 (2-cup) servings

Nutrients per Serving: Calories: 258, Carbohydrate: 25g, Total Fat: 9g, Saturated Fat: 4g, Fiber: 5g

old-fashioned beef stew

1½ pounds beef top or bottom round steak, trimmed

3 teaspoons olive oil, divided

4 cups sliced mushrooms

2 cloves garlic, minced

2 cups baby carrots

2 cups fat-free reduced-sodium beef broth

2 tablespoons tomato paste

¾ teaspoon dried thyme

½ teaspoon salt

½ teaspoon black pepper

2 bay leaves

2 medium onions, cut into wedges

2 cups frozen cut green beans

3 tablespoons water

3 tablespoons all-purpose flour

1. Cut beef into 1-inch cubes. Heat 2 teaspoons oil in Dutch oven over medium-high heat. Brown beef in 2 batches; remove from pan.

2. Heat remaining 1 teaspoon oil in same pan. Add mushrooms; cook and stir until browned. Add garlic; cook and stir 30 seconds. Add beef, carrots, broth, tomato paste, thyme, salt, pepper and bay leaves. Bring to a boil; cover and reduce heat. Simmer about 2 hours or until beef is tender. Add onions and green beans during last 30 minutes of cooking.

3. Stir water into flour in small bowl. Stir mixture into stew; simmer 2 to 3 minutes to thicken.   Makes 6 (1⅓-cup) servings

Nutrients per Serving: Calories: 240, Carbohydrate: 18g, Total Fat: 5g, Saturated Fat: 2g, Fiber: 5g

lettuce wrap enchiladas

Nonstick cooking spray

2 bell peppers, cut into ¼-inch strips

2 tablespoons water

1 ½ teaspoons chili powder

1 cup shredded cooked chicken

½ cup fresh cilantro, chopped

Romaine lettuce leaves

½ cup fat-free refried beans, warmed

½ cup salsa

½ cup (2 ounces) reduced-fat shredded Cheddar cheese

¼ cup fat-free sour cream

1. Lightly spray large skillet with cooking spray. Heat over medium-high heat. Add pepper strips, water and chili powder. Cook 4 to 5 minutes or until water evaporates, stirring occasionally. Reduce heat to low. Add chicken; heat until warm. Stir in cilantro; cover and keep warm.

2. Make 4 enchilada wrappers by arranging lettuce leaves to make cup shapes.

3. Spread each wrapper with one fourth of beans and one fourth of chicken mixture. Top each with 2 tablespoons salsa, 2 tablespoons cheese and 1 tablespoon sour cream.

Makes 2 servings (2 enchiladas per serving)

Nutrients per Serving: Calories: 290, Carbohydrate: 21g, Total Fat: 9g, Saturated Fat: 4g, Fiber: 6g

salmon black bean patties

1 can (7½ ounces) pink salmon, drained
½ cup black beans, rinsed and drained
¼ cup dry bread crumbs
¼ cup sliced green onions
1 egg white
1 tablespoon chopped fresh cilantro
1 tablespoon lime juice
Pinch ground red pepper or seafood seasoning mix
Salt and black pepper
1 tablespoon canola oil

1. Place salmon in medium bowl. Shred with fork.

2. Add beans, bread crumbs, green onions, egg white, cilantro, lime juice and red pepper to bowl. Season with salt and pepper. Gently stir to combine. Shape mixture into 3 patties about 1¼ inches thick. Refrigerate 30 minutes or until ready to cook.

3. Heat oil in large skillet over medium heat. Cook patties 2 to 3 minutes per side or until firm and brown.

Makes 3 servings

serving suggestion: Serve with grilled eggplant slices and your favorite salsa. Garnish with cilantro sprigs and lime wedges, if desired.

Nutrients per Serving: Calories: 205, Carbohydrate: 13g, Total Fat: 10g, Saturated Fat: 2g, Fiber: 3g

hoisin beef stir-fry

    3 tablespoons hoisin sauce

       Grated peel and juice from 1 medium orange

    1 tablespoon cider vinegar

    ⅛ to ¼ teaspoon red pepper flakes

    ¼ cup slivered almonds

       Nonstick cooking spray

    ½ teaspoon dark sesame oil

    1 medium red bell pepper, cut into strips

    4 cups packaged coleslaw mix or shredded cabbage

    ¼ teaspoon salt

    1½ cups snow peas (3 ounces)

    12 ounces sirloin steak, cut into thin strips

1. Combine hoisin sauce, orange peel and juice, vinegar and red pepper flakes in small bowl. Set aside.

2. Heat large nonstick skillet over medium-high heat. Add almonds; cook and stir 2 minutes or until beginning to lightly brown. Remove to plate to cool.

3. Coat skillet with cooking spray; add sesame oil. Add bell peppers; cook and stir 2 minutes. Add coleslaw and salt; cook and stir 2 minutes. Transfer to serving dish.

4. Coat skillet with cooking spray. Add snow peas; cook and stir 2 minutes or until crisp-tender. Transfer to serving dish with coleslaw; keep warm.

5. Coat skillet with cooking spray. Add steak; cook and stir 2 minutes. Arrange on top of vegetables; keep warm.

6. Add hoisin mixture to skillet. Cook and stir 2 minutes or until sauce reduces to ¼ cup. Spoon over steak. Sprinkle with almonds.

Makes 4 servings

Nutrients per Serving: Calories: 236, Carbohydrate: 14g, Total Fat: 12g, Saturated Fat: 3g, Fiber: 3g

grilled fish tacos

¾ teaspoon chili powder

1 pound skinless mahi mahi, halibut or tilapia fillets

½ cup salsa, divided

2 cups packaged coleslaw mix or shredded cabbage

¼ cup reduced-fat sour cream

¼ cup chopped fresh cilantro, divided

8 (6-inch) corn tortillas, warmed according to package directions

1. Prepare grill for direct cooking. Sprinkle chili powder over fish. Spoon ¼ cup salsa over fish; let stand 10 minutes. Meanwhile, combine coleslaw mix, remaining ¼ cup salsa, sour cream and 2 tablespoons cilantro in large bowl; mix well.

2. Grill fish, salsa side up, over medium coals, covered, 8 to 10 minutes without turning or until fish is opaque in center. Slice fish crosswise into thin strips or cut into chunks. Fill warm tortillas with fish and coleslaw mix. Garnish with remaining cilantro.   **Makes 4 servings**

Nutrients per Serving: Calories: 243, Carbohydrate: 28g, Total Fat: 4g, Saturated Fat: 1g, Fiber: 5g

TIP

Fish is an excellent choice for healthy eating and it's a quick and easy dinner as well. Fish fillets cook in a matter of minutes and the delicate flavor takes well to any number of seasonings. mahi mahi, like all fish, has a GI and glycemic load of zero. In addition, it is a good source of niacin and other B vitamins.

southwestern chicken & black bean skillet

1 teaspoon ground cumin

1 teaspoon chili powder

½ teaspoon salt

4 boneless skinless chicken breasts (4 ounces each)

2 teaspoons canola or vegetable oil

1 cup chopped onion

1 red bell pepper, chopped

1 can (about 15 ounces) black beans, rinsed and drained

½ cup chunky salsa

¼ cup chopped fresh cilantro or thinly sliced green onions (optional)

1. Combine cumin, chili powder and salt in small bowl; sprinkle evenly over both sides of chicken. Heat oil in large nonstick skillet over medium-high heat. Add chicken; cook 2 minutes per side. Transfer chicken to plate.

2. Add onion to skillet; cook and stir 1 minute. Add bell pepper; cook over medium heat 5 minutes, stirring occasionally. Stir in beans and salsa.

3. Place chicken over bean mixture. Cover and cook 6 to 7 minutes or until chicken is no longer pink in center. Garnish with cilantro.

Makes 4 servings

Nutrients per Serving: Calories: 262, Carbohydrate: 22g, Total Fat: 4g, Saturated Fat: <1g, Fiber: 7g

greek chickpea salad

4 cups packed baby spinach leaves

1 cup canned chickpeas, rinsed and drained

4 pitted kalamata olives, sliced

1 large shallot, thinly sliced

2 tablespoons crumbled reduced-fat feta cheese

dressing

¼ cup plain fat-free Greek yogurt

2 teaspoons white wine vinegar

1 clove garlic, minced

1 teaspoon olive oil

¼ teaspoon pepper

⅛ teaspoon salt

1. Combine spinach, chickpeas, olives, shallot and feta in large salad bowl. Toss gently.

2. For dressing, stir together yogurt, vinegar, garlic, oil, pepper and salt in small bowl. Spoon dressing over salad just before serving. Toss gently.

Makes 4 to 5 (1-cup) servings

Nutrients per Serving: Calories: 115, Carbohydrate: 17g, Total Fat: 3g, Saturated Fat: 1g, Fiber: 4g

wilted spinach salad with white beans & olives

    2 thick slices bacon, diced
½ cup chopped onion
    1 can (about 15 ounces) navy beans, rinsed and drained
½ cup halved pitted kalamata or ripe olives
    1 package (9 ounces) baby spinach
    1 cup cherry tomatoes (cut in half if large)
1½ tablespoons balsamic vinegar
    Black pepper

1. Cook bacon in Dutch oven or large saucepan over medium heat
2 minutes. Add onion; cook, stirring occasionally, 5 to 6 minutes or until
bacon is crisp and onion is tender. Stir in beans and olives; heat through.

2. Add spinach, tomatoes and vinegar; cover and cook 1 minute or until
spinach is slightly wilted. Turn off heat; toss lightly. Transfer to serving
plates. Season with pepper.   Makes 4 (1¾-cup) servings

Nutrients per Serving: Calories: 230, Carbohydrate: 35g, Total Fat: 5g,
Saturated Fat: 1g, Fiber: 14g

TIP
Eating more beans may be the
tastiest, easiest way to add fiber,
protein and vitamins to your low GI
eating plan. They are economical,
convenient and available in a
rainbow of colors and a range of
sizes. There are heirloom beans,
pink beans, turtle beans, black
beans and many more. In most
recipes one variety may easily be
substituted for another.

main-dish mediterranean salad

1 package (10 ounces) ready-to-use chopped romaine lettuce

½ pound fresh green beans, cooked and drained or 1 can (about 14 ounces) whole green beans, drained

1 pouch (5½ ounces) solid white tuna, flaked

8 ounces cherry tomatoes, halved

dressing

2 tablespoons olive oil

2 tablespoons cider vinegar or white vinegar

1½ teaspoons Dijon mustard

½ teaspoon black pepper

1. Place lettuce, green beans, tuna and tomatoes in large bowl.

2. For dressing, whisk oil, vinegar, mustard and pepper in small bowl until blended. Pour dressing over salad; toss well. Serve immediately.

Makes 4 (3-cup) servings

Nutrients per Serving: Calories: 156, Carbohydrate: 9g, Total Fat: 8g, Saturated Fat: 1g, Fiber: 4g

TIP

Since the presence of an acid or fat in a meal lowers the GI of the carbohydrate, dressing is an important part of a salad. If you've ever been on a diet that forbade salad dressing, you'll cheer this good news. Learn to make a simple vinaigrette, like the one in this recipe, for all your salads. Keep it stored in a shaker jar in your refrigerator. That way you won't be tempted by store-bought dressings that are often loaded with sugary, starchy ingredients and preservatives.

black bean & bell pepper burritos

2 teaspoons canola oil

1½ cups diced red, yellow and green bell peppers or 1 large green bell pepper, diced

½ cup chopped onion

1 can (about 15 ounces) black beans, rinsed and drained

½ cup salsa

1 teaspoon chili powder

7 (8-inch) whole wheat or multigrain low-carb flour tortillas, warmed

¾ cup (3 ounces) reduced-fat shredded Cheddar or Mexican cheese blend

½ cup chopped fresh cilantro

1. Heat oil in large nonstick skillet over medium heat. Add bell peppers and onion. Cover; cook 3 to 4 minutes. Add beans, salsa and chili powder. Cover; simmer 5 minutes. Uncover; simmer 3 minutes or until vegetables are tender and sauce thickens, stirring occasionally.

2. Spoon about ⅔ cup bean mixture down center of each tortilla. Top with cheese and cilantro. Fold outer edges of tortillas over filling; roll up.

Makes 7 servings

Nutrients per Serving: Calories: 170, Carbohydrate: 31g, Total Fat: 4g, Saturated Fat: <1g, Fiber: 6g

spring greens with blueberries, walnuts & feta cheese

1 tablespoon canola oil

1 tablespoon white wine vinegar or sherry vinegar

2 teaspoons Dijon mustard

½ teaspoon salt

½ teaspoon black pepper

5 cups mixed spring greens (5 ounces)

1 cup fresh blueberries

½ cup reduced-fat crumbled feta cheese

¼ cup chopped walnuts or pecans, toasted*

To toast nuts, place in nonstick skillet. Cook and stir over medium-low heat until nuts begin to brown, about 5 minutes. Remove immediately to plate to cool.

1. Whisk together oil, vinegar, mustard, salt and pepper in large bowl.

2. Add greens and blueberries; toss gently to coat. Serve immediately.

Makes 4 (1¼-cup) servings

Nutrients per Serving: Calories: 146, Carbohydrate: 8g, Total Fat: 11g, Saturated Fat: 2g, Fiber: 3g

TIP

It's usually best to dress salads at the last minute so the greens don't wilt. If you will not be serving the salad immediately, combine the dressing ingredients in a small jar with a tight fitting lid. Shake to combine the ingredients right before serving and dress the salad at the table.

chunky italian stew with white beans

1 teaspoon extra virgin olive oil

2 green bell peppers, cut into ¾-inch pieces

1 yellow squash, cut into ¾-inch pieces

1 zucchini, cut into ¾-inch pieces

1 onion, cut into ¾-inch pieces

4 ounces mushrooms, quartered (about 1 cup)

1 can (about 14 ounces) diced tomatoes

1 teaspoon dried oregano

½ teaspoon sugar

½ teaspoon Italian seasoning

⅛ teaspoon red pepper flakes (optional)

Salt and black pepper

1 can (about 15 ounces) navy beans, rinsed and drained

¾ cup (3 ounces) shredded part-skim mozzarella cheese

1 tablespoon grated Parmesan cheese

1. Heat oil in Dutch oven or large saucepan over medium-high heat. Add bell peppers, squash, zucchini, onion and mushrooms. Cook and stir 8 minutes or until onions are translucent. Stir in tomatoes, oregano, sugar, Italian seasoning and red pepper flakes, if desired. Season with salt and pepper. Reduce heat; cover and simmer 15 minutes or until vegetables are tender, stirring once.

2. Remove Dutch oven from heat. Stir in beans; let stand, covered, 5 minutes. Top with cheeses. Makes 4 (1½-cup) servings

Nutrients per Serving: Calories: 265, Carbohydrate: 38g, Total Fat: 6g, Saturated Fat: 3g, Fiber: 9g

healthy chopped salad

10 ounces cooked skinless turkey breast, chopped
1 small head bok choy, chopped
2 cups baby spinach, chopped
1 tomato, chopped
1 cup baby carrots, chopped
1 package (8 ounces) sugar snap peas, chopped
2 romaine lettuce hearts, chopped
Juice of 1 lemon (about ¼ cup)
Juice of 1 lime (about ¼ cup)
1 tablespoon creamy peanut butter
2 teaspoons sugar substitute*
2 teaspoons sesame seeds
1 teaspoon minced garlic
Salt and black pepper

*This recipe was tested with sucralose-based sugar substitute.

1. Place turkey, bok choy, spinach, tomato, carrots, peas and romaine in large bowl.

2. For dressing, combine lemon juice, lime juice, peanut butter, sugar substitute, sesame seeds, garlic, salt and pepper in small jar with tight-fitting lid; shake until well blended.

3. Pour dressing over salad; toss well.   Makes 8 servings

serving suggestion: For an elegant presentation, instead of tossing the salad in a bowl, arrange lines of the chopped ingredients across a large serving platter. Toss the salad at the table on the platter, or leave it untossed and let guests select their favorite mix of ingredients. Pass the dressing at the table.

Nutrients per Serving: Calories: 96, Carbohydrate: 7g, Total Fat: 2g, Saturated Fat: <1g, Fiber: 2g

mediterranean barley-bean salad

⅔ cup pearl barley

3 cups asparagus pieces

2 cans (about 15 ounces each) dark red kidney beans, rinsed and drained

2 tablespoons chopped fresh mint

¼ cup lemon juice

¼ cup fat-free Italian salad dressing

¼ teaspoon black pepper

Kale leaves (optional)

¼ cup dry-roasted sunflower seeds

1. Cook barley according to package directions, omitting salt and fat. Add asparagus to barley during last 5 minutes of cooking time. Drain; transfer to large bowl. Refrigerate at least 2 hours.

2. Stir beans and mint into barley mixture. Whisk together lemon juice, salad dressing and pepper in small bowl. Drizzle over barley mixture. Serve on kale leaves, if desired. Sprinkle with sunflower kernels.

Makes 4 (2-cup) servings

Nutrients per Serving: Calories: 377, Carbohydrate: 68g, Total Fat: 5g, Saturated Fat: 1g, Fiber: 22g

barley & swiss chard skillet casserole

1 cup water
¾ cup quick-cooking barley
1 cup chopped red bell pepper
1 cup chopped green bell pepper
⅛ teaspoon garlic powder
⅛ teaspoon red pepper flakes
2 cups packed coarsely chopped Swiss chard leaves*
1 cup canned navy beans, rinsed and drained
1 cup quartered cherry tomatoes
¼ cup chopped fresh basil leaves
1 tablespoon olive oil
2 tablespoons Italian-seasoned dry bread crumbs

Fresh spinach or beet greens can be substituted for Swiss chard.

1. Preheat broiler.

2. Bring water to a boil in large ovenproof skillet; add barley, bell peppers, garlic powder and red pepper flakes. Reduce heat; cover tightly and simmer 10 minutes or until liquid is absorbed.

3. Remove skillet from heat. Stir in chard, beans, tomatoes, basil and olive oil. Sprinkle evenly with bread crumbs. Broil, uncovered, 2 minutes or until golden. Makes 4 (1¼-cup) servings

Nutrients per Serving: Calories: 288, Carbohydrate: 45g, Total Fat: 6g, Saturated Fat: <1g, Fiber: 12g

6-bean party salad

2 romaine lettuce hearts

1 can (about 8 ounces) lima beans, rinsed and drained

1 can (about 15 ounces) pinto beans, rinsed and drained

1 can (about 15 ounces) dark red kidney beans, rinsed and drained

1 can (about 15 ounces) chickpeas, rinsed and drained

1 can (about 15 ounces) black beans, rinsed and drained

1 can (about 15 ounces) pigeon peas, rinsed and drained

½ cup reduced-fat Italian salad dressing

1. Set aside 10 romaine lettuce leaves for garnish. Thinly slice remaining lettuce; place in large bowl.

2. Add beans and dressing to lettuce. Toss gently.

3. Stand lettuce leaf upright in each of 10 glasses. Spoon 1 cup salad mixture into each glass. **Makes 10 servings**

Nutrients per Serving: Calories: 224, Carbohydrate: 40g, Total Fat: 2g, Saturated Fat: <1g, Fiber: 11g

TIP
Cooking dried beans instead of using canned takes a little time, but it's easy and even more economical. You'll also find that beans cooked from dry usually have better flavor and a firmer texture. Buy dried beans from a market that has a good turnover, such as a Latin American one, since dried beans that have been on the shelf for a long time take much longer to cook. Follow the recipe on the bag of beans or one from any basic cookbook. Once the beans are cooked, portions can easily be frozen for later use.

roasted vegetable salad

1 cup sliced mushrooms

1 cup sliced carrots

1 cup chopped green or yellow bell pepper

1 cup cherry tomatoes, halved

½ cup chopped onion

2 tablespoons chopped pitted kalamata olives

2 teaspoons lemon juice, divided

1 teaspoon dried oregano

1 teaspoon olive oil

½ teaspoon black pepper

1 teaspoon sugar substitute (optional)

3 cups packed baby spinach

1. Preheat oven to 375°F. Combine mushrooms, carrots, bell pepper, tomatoes, onion, olives, 1 teaspoon lemon juice, oregano, oil and black pepper in large bowl; toss until evenly coated.

2. Spread vegetables in single layer on baking sheet. Bake 20 minutes, stirring once. Stir in remaining 1 teaspoon lemon juice and sugar substitute, if desired. Serve warm over spinach.   **Makes 2 servings**

Nutrients per Serving: Calories: 121, Carbohydrate: 20g, Total Fat: 4g, Saturated Fat: <1g, Fiber: 6g

bulgur pilaf with tomato & zucchini

1 cup uncooked bulgur wheat

1 tablespoon olive oil

¾ cup chopped onion

2 cloves garlic, minced

½ pound zucchini (2 small), thinly sliced

1 can (about 14 ounces) whole tomatoes, drained and coarsely chopped

1 cup fat-free reduced-sodium chicken or vegetable broth

1 teaspoon dried basil

⅛ teaspoon black pepper

1. Rinse bulgur thoroughly in colander under cold water; drain well.

2. Heat oil in large saucepan over medium heat. Add onion and garlic; cook and stir 3 minutes or until onion is tender. Stir in zucchini and tomatoes; reduce heat to medium-low. Cook, covered, 15 minutes or until zucchini is almost tender, stirring occasionally.

3. Stir broth, bulgur, basil and pepper into vegetable mixture. Bring to a boil over high heat. Cover; remove from heat. Let stand 10 minutes or until liquid is absorbed. Stir gently before serving.   **Makes 8 servings**

Nutrients per Serving: Calories: 98, Carbohydrate: 18g, Total Fat: 2g, Saturated Fat: <1g, Fiber: 5g

spinach artichoke gratin

2 cups (16 ounces) fat-free cottage cheese

½ cup cholesterol-free egg substitute

4½ tablespoons grated Parmesan cheese, divided

1 tablespoon lemon juice

⅛ teaspoon black pepper

⅛ teaspoon ground nutmeg

2 packages (10 ounces each) frozen chopped spinach, thawed

⅓ cup thinly sliced green onions

1 package (10 ounces) frozen artichoke hearts, thawed and halved

1. Preheat oven to 375°F. Coat 1½-quart baking dish with nonstick cooking spray.

2. Process cottage cheese, egg substitute, 3 tablespoons Parmesan cheese, lemon juice, pepper and nutmeg in food processor until smooth.

3. Squeeze moisture from spinach. Combine spinach, cottage cheese mixture and green onions in large bowl. Spread half of mixture in baking dish.

4. Pat artichoke halves dry with paper towels. Place in single layer over spinach mixture. Sprinkle with remaining Parmesan cheese. Cover with remaining spinach mixture. Bake, covered, 25 minutes.

Makes 6 (1-cup) servings

Nutrients per Serving: Calories: 125, Carbohydrate: 13g, Total Fat: 1g, Saturated Fat: <1g, Fiber: 5g

light greek spanakopita

    Olive oil nonstick cooking spray
1 teaspoon olive oil
1 large onion, cut into quarters and sliced
2 cloves garlic, minced
1 package (10 ounces) frozen chopped spinach, thawed and
    squeezed dry
½ cup reduced-fat feta cheese crumbles
5 sheets phyllo dough, thawed
½ cup cholesterol-free egg substitute
¼ teaspoon nutmeg
¼ to ½ teaspoon black pepper
⅛ teaspoon salt

1. Preheat oven to 375°F. Spray 8-inch square baking pan with cooking spray.

2. Heat oil in large skillet over medium heat. Add onion; cook and stir 7 to 8 minutes or until soft. Add garlic; cook and stir 30 seconds. Add spinach and cheese; cook and stir until spinach is heated through.

3. Place 1 sheet phyllo dough on counter with long side toward you. (Cover remaining phyllo with damp towel until needed.) Spray right half of phyllo with cooking spray; fold left half over sprayed half. Place sheet in prepared pan. (Two edges will hang over sides of pan.) Spray top of sheet. Spray and fold 2 more sheets of phyllo the same way. Place sheets into pan at 90° angles so edges will hang over all 4 sides of pan. Spray each sheet after it is placed in pan.

4. Combine egg substitute, nutmeg, pepper and salt in small bowl. Stir into spinach mixture. Spread filling over phyllo in pan. Spray and fold 1 sheet of phyllo as above; place on top of filling, tucking ends under filling. Bring all overhanging edges of phyllo over top sheet; spray lightly. Spray and fold last sheet as above; place over top sheet, tucking ends under. Spray lightly. Bake 25 to 27 minutes or until top is barely browned. Cool 10 to 15 minutes before serving.   **Makes 4 servings**

Nutrients per Serving: Calories: 172, Carbohydrate: 18g, Total Fat: 6g, Saturated Fat: 2g, Fiber: 3g

thai chicken broccoli salad

4 ounces uncooked linguine

Nonstick cooking spray

½ pound boneless skinless chicken breasts, cut into bite-size pieces

2 cups broccoli florets

2 tablespoons cold water

⅔ cup chopped red bell pepper

6 green onions, sliced diagonally into 1-inch pieces

¼ cup reduced-fat creamy peanut butter

2 tablespoons hot water

2 tablespoons reduced-sodium soy sauce

2 teaspoons dark sesame oil

½ teaspoon red pepper flakes

⅛ teaspoon garlic powder

¼ cup unsalted peanuts, chopped

1. Cook pasta according to package directions; drain.

2. Spray large nonstick skillet with cooking spray; heat over medium-high heat. Add chicken; stir-fry 5 minutes or until chicken is cooked through. Transfer chicken to large bowl.

3. Add broccoli and cold water to skillet. Cook, covered, 2 minutes over medium-high heat. Uncover; cook and stir 2 minutes or until broccoli is crisp-tender. Transfer broccoli to bowl with chicken. Add pasta, bell pepper and onions.

4. Combine peanut butter, hot water, soy sauce, oil, red pepper flakes and garlic powder in small bowl until well blended. Drizzle over salad; toss to coat. Top with peanuts before serving.   **Makes 4 servings**

Nutrients per Serving: Calories: 275, Carbohydrate: 29g, Total Fat: 9g, Saturated Fat: 2g, Fiber: 4g

grilled tuna niçoise with citrus marinade

      Citrus Marinade (recipe follows)
   1 tuna steak (about 1 pound)
   2 cups fresh green beans
   4 cups romaine lettuce leaves, washed and torn
   8 small red potatoes, cooked and quartered
   1 cup chopped seeded fresh tomato
   4 cooked egg whites, chopped
   ¼ cup red onion slices, halved
   2 teaspoons chopped black olives
      Prepared salad dressing (optional)

1. Prepare Citrus Marinade. Place tuna in large resealable food storage bag; add marinade. Seal bag; turn to coat. Marinate in refrigerator 1 hour, turning occasionally.

2. Prepare grill for direct cooking. Drain tuna; discard marinade. Grill 8 to 10 minutes or until tuna begins to flake when tested with fork, turning once. (Or, broil tuna 4 inches from heat, 8 to 10 minutes, turning once.) Slice tuna into ¼-inch-thick slices; set aside.

3. Place 2 cups water in large saucepan; bring to a boil over high heat. Add beans; cook 2 minutes. Drain; rinse with cold water and drain again.

4. Place lettuce on large serving platter. Arrange tuna slices, beans, potatoes, tomato, egg whites and onion on lettuce. Sprinkle with olives. Serve with salad dressing, if desired.   **Makes 4 servings**

citrus marinade: Combine ½ cup lime juice, ¼ cup vegetable oil, 2 chopped green onions, 1 teaspoon dried tarragon, ¼ teaspoon garlic powder and ¼ teaspoon black pepper in small bowl.

Nutrients per Serving: Calories: 373, Carbohydrate: 45g, Total Fat: 7g, Saturated Fat: 1g, Fiber: 6g

overstuffed peppers, mexican style

10 ounces 95% lean ground beef

½ cup finely chopped onion

1 can (4 ounces) chopped mild green chiles

½ cup frozen corn

¼ cup cornmeal

½ cup tomato sauce, divided

½ teaspoon ground cumin

½ teaspoon salt

2 large green bell peppers, cut in half lengthwise, seeded and stemmed

2 ounces (½ cup) shredded reduced-fat sharp Cheddar cheese

1. Preheat oven to 375°F.

2. Brown beef in medium nonstick skillet over medium-high heat 6 to 8 minutes, stirring to break up meat. Drain fat. Add onion, chiles, corn, cornmeal, ¼ cup tomato sauce, cumin and salt. Mix well.

3. Arrange pepper halves, cut side up, in 12×8-inch baking pan. Spoon beef mixture into each. Spoon remaining ¼ cup tomato sauce over each pepper half. Bake about 35 minutes or until peppers are tender.

4. Sprinkle each pepper half with cheese.   Makes 4 servings

Nutrients per Serving: Calories: 232, Carbohydrate: 19g, Total Fat: 8g, Saturated Fat: 5g, Fiber: 4g

chicken, hummus & vegetable wraps

¾ cup hummus (regular, roasted red bell pepper or roasted garlic)

4 (8- to 10-inch) sun-dried tomato or spinach wraps or whole wheat tortillas

2 cups chopped cooked chicken breast

Chipotle hot sauce or Louisiana-style hot sauce (optional)

½ cup shredded carrots

½ cup chopped unpeeled cucumber

½ cup thinly sliced radishes

2 tablespoons chopped fresh mint or basil

Spread hummus evenly over wraps all the way to edges. Arrange chicken over hummus; sprinkle with hot sauce, if desired. Top with carrots, cucumber, radishes and mint. Roll up tightly. Cut in half diagonally.

Makes 4 servings

variation: Substitute alfalfa sprouts for the radishes.

Nutrients per Serving: Calories: 308, Carbohydrate: 32g, Total Fat: 10g, Saturated Fat: 1g, Fiber: 15g

TIP

Wraps are a great substitute for sandwich bread when you're eating low GI. Instead of two slices of starchy white bread, tuck fillings into one of the many flavorful varieties of tortillas that are now readily available. Rich, creamy hummus, which is made of chickpeas, is a great low-GI spread that provides some fiber. (See page 116 for a recipe for homemade hummus.)

mediterranean soup with mozzarella

Nonstick cooking spray
2 medium green bell peppers, chopped
1 cup chopped onion
2 cups (about 8 ounces) chopped eggplant
1 cup (about 4 ounces) sliced mushrooms
2 cloves garlic, minced
6 teaspoons dried basil, divided
3 cups water
1 can (about 14 ounces) diced tomatoes with Italian herbs
½ cup red wine or water
1 can (about 15 ounces) white beans, rinsed and drained
2 teaspoons sugar
¼ teaspoon salt
1½ cups (6 ounces) shredded reduced-fat mozzarella cheese
¼ cup minced fresh parsley

1. Spray Dutch oven with cooking spray; heat over medium-high heat. Add bell peppers and onion; cook 4 minutes or until onion is translucent, stirring frequently.

2. Add eggplant, mushrooms, garlic and 5 teaspoons basil. Cook and stir 4 minutes. Stir in water, tomatoes and wine. Reduce heat; cover and simmer 30 minutes, stirring occasionally.

3. Remove from heat. Stir in beans, sugar and salt. Cover and let stand 5 minutes. Toss remaining 1 teaspoon basil with cheese and parsley in small bowl; top each serving with cheese mixture.   Makes 6 servings

Nutrients per Serving: Calories: 130, Carbohydrate: 9g, Total Fat: 3g, Saturated Fat: 1g, Fiber: 2g

spring vegetable ragoût

1 tablespoon olive oil

2 leeks, thinly sliced

3 cloves garlic, minced

1 cup vegetable broth

1 package (10 ounces) frozen corn

½ pound yellow squash, halved lengthwise and cut into ½-inch pieces (about 1¼ cups)

1 small bag (6 ounces) frozen edamame (soybeans), shelled

1 small bag (4 ounces) shredded carrots

3 cups cherry tomatoes, halved

1 teaspoon dried tarragon

1 teaspoon dried basil

1 teaspoon dried oregano

Salt and black pepper

Minced fresh parsley (optional)

1. Heat oil in large skillet over medium heat. Add leeks and garlic; cook and stir just until fragrant. Add broth, corn, squash, edamame and carrots; cook, stirring occasionally, until squash is tender.

2. Add tomatoes, tarragon, basil and oregano; stir well. Reduce heat and simmer, covered, 2 minutes or until tomatoes are soft.

3. Season with salt and pepper. Garnish with parsley.

Makes 6 servings

Nutrients per Serving: Calories: 156, Carbohydrate: 25g, Total Fat: 5g, Saturated Fat: <1g, Fiber: 5g

blt cukes

½ cup finely chopped lettuce

½ cup finely chopped spinach

3 slices bacon, crisp-cooked and crumbled

¼ cup finely diced tomato

1 tablespoon plus 1½ teaspoons fat-free mayonnaise

¼ teaspoon black pepper

⅛ teaspoon salt

1 large cucumber

Minced fresh parsley or green onion (optional)

1. Combine lettuce, spinach, bacon, tomato, mayonnaise, pepper and salt in medium bowl; mix well.

2. Peel cucumber; trim off ends and cut in half lengthwise. Use spoon to scoop out seeds; discard seeds.

3. Divide bacon mixture between cucumber halves, mounding in center. Garnish with parsley. Cut into 2-inch pieces.   **Makes 8 to 10 pieces**

tip: Make these snacks when cucumbers are plentiful and large enough to easily hollow out with a spoon. These snacks can be made, covered and refrigerated up to 12 hours ahead of time.

Nutrients per Serving: Calories: 26, Carbohydrate: 2g, Total Fat: 2g, Saturated Fat: <1g, Fiber: <1g

tuna tabbouleh salad

1 cup water

¾ cup uncooked fine-grain bulgur wheat

1 teaspoon grated lemon peel

3 tablespoons lemon juice

1 small clove garlic, minced

½ teaspoon salt

⅛ teaspoon black pepper

1 tablespoon olive oil

1 cup red or yellow cherry tomatoes (quartered if large)

1 cup chopped cucumber

¼ cup finely chopped red onion

3 cans (5 ounces each) chunk white albacore tuna packed in water, drained and flaked

½ cup chopped Italian parsley

4 cups watercress, tough stems removed

1. Bring water to a boil in small saucepan. Remove from heat and add bulgur. Cover and let stand 15 minutes. Place bulgur in fine mesh sieve. Run under cold water to cool; drain thoroughly.

2. Meanwhile, whisk together lemon peel, lemon juice, garlic, salt and pepper in large bowl. Slowly whisk in olive oil. Add tomatoes, cucumber, onion and bulgur; stir to combine. Gently stir in tuna and parsley. Arrange watercress on 4 serving plates; spoon about 1½ cups salad onto each plate. Makes 4 servings

Nutrients per Serving: Calories: 282, Carbohydrate: 22g, Total Fat: 8g, Saturated Fat: 1g, Fiber: 4g

individual spinach & bacon quiches

3 slices bacon

½ small onion, diced

1 package (10 ounces) frozen chopped spinach, thawed and squeezed dry

½ teaspoon black pepper

⅛ teaspoon ground nutmeg

Pinch salt

1 container (15 ounces) whole milk ricotta cheese

2 cups (8 ounces) shredded mozzarella cheese

1 cup grated Parmesan cheese

3 eggs, lightly beaten

1. Preheat oven to 350°F. Spray 10 standard (2½-inch) muffin cups with nonstick cooking spray.

2. Cook bacon in large skillet over medium-high heat until crisp. Drain on paper towels. Let bacon cool; crumble.

3. In same skillet, cook and stir onion 5 minutes or until tender. Add spinach, pepper, nutmeg and salt. Cook and stir over medium heat about 3 minutes or until liquid evaporates. Remove from heat. Stir in bacon; cool.

4. Combine cheeses in large bowl. Add eggs; stir until well blended. Add cooled spinach mixture; mix well.

5. Divide mixture evenly among prepared muffin cups. Bake 40 minutes or until set. Let stand 10 minutes. Run knife around edges to release. Serve hot or refrigerate and serve cold.   **Makes 10 servings**

Nutrients per Serving: Calories: 216, Carbohydrate: 4g, Total Fat: 15g, Saturated Fat: 9g, Fiber: 1g

rosemary-scented nut mix

2 tablespoons unsalted butter

2 cups pecan halves

1 cup unsalted macadamia nuts

1 cup walnuts

1 teaspoon dried rosemary

½ teaspoon salt

¼ teaspoon red pepper flakes

1. Preheat oven to 300°F. Melt butter in large saucepan over low heat. Add pecans, macadamia nuts and walnuts; mix well. Add rosemary, salt and red pepper flakes; cook and stir about 1 minute.

2. Spread mixture on ungreased nonstick baking sheet. Bake 15 minutes, stirring occasionally. Cool completely on baking sheet on wire rack.

Makes 16 (¼-cup) servings

Nutrients per Serving: Calories: 216, Carbohydrate: 4g, Total Fat: 22g, Saturated Fat: 4g, Fiber: 2g

mediterranean roasted tomatoes

2 medium beefsteak tomatoes, cut in half crosswise

4 fresh basil leaves

2 tablespoons finely chopped pitted kalamata olives

2 tablespoons shredded reduced-fat mozzarella cheese

2 tablespoons grated Parmesan cheese

1. Preheat toaster oven or oven to broil. Place tomato halves on rack of toaster oven tray or broiler pan. Top each tomato half with 1 fresh basil leaf and one fourth of olives and cheeses.

2. Broil 2 minutes or until cheese melts and begins to brown. Let cool slightly before serving.

Makes 4 servings

Nutrients per Serving: Calories: 34, Carbohydrate: 3g, Total Fat: 2g, Saturated Fat: 1g, Fiber: 1g

chicken & spinach quesadillas with pico de gallo

2 cups chopped seeded tomatoes (2 medium), divided
1 cup chopped green onions, divided
½ cup minced fresh cilantro
1 tablespoon minced jalapeño pepper*
1 tablespoon fresh lime juice
1 cup packed chopped stemmed spinach
1 cup shredded cooked boneless skinless chicken breast
10 (8-inch) fat-free flour tortillas
Nonstick cooking spray
¾ cup (3 ounces) shredded reduced-fat Cheddar cheese

Jalapeño peppers can sting and irritate the skin, so wear rubber gloves when handling peppers and do not touch your eyes.

1. For pico de gallo, combine 1½ cups tomatoes, ¾ cup green onions, cilantro, jalapeño and lime juice in medium bowl; set aside.

2. Divide remaining ½ cup tomatoes, ¼ cup green onions, spinach and chicken among 5 tortillas; sprinkle with cheese. Top with remaining 5 tortillas.

3. Spray large nonstick skillet with cooking spray. Cook quesadillas, one at a time, over medium heat 2 minutes per side or until lightly browned and cheese is melted. Cut into wedges and serve with pico de gallo.

Makes 5 servings

Nutrients per Serving: Calories: 240, Carbohydrate: 32g, Total Fat: 5g, Saturated Fat: 5g, Fiber: 14g

asian vegetable rolls with soy-lime dipping sauce

¼ cup soy sauce

2 tablespoons lime juice

1 clove garlic, crushed

1 teaspoon honey

½ teaspoon finely chopped fresh ginger

¼ teaspoon dark sesame oil

⅛ to ¼ teaspoon red pepper flakes

½ cup grated cucumber

⅓ cup grated carrot

¼ cup sliced yellow bell pepper

2 tablespoons thinly sliced green onion

18 small lettuce leaves

Sesame seeds (optional)

1. Combine soy sauce, lime juice, garlic, honey, ginger, oil and red pepper flakes in small bowl. Combine cucumber, carrot, bell pepper and green onion in medium bowl. Stir 1 tablespoon soy sauce mixture into vegetable mixture.

2. Place about 1 tablespoon vegetable mixture on each lettuce leaf. Roll up leaves; sprinkle with sesame seeds, if desired. Serve with remaining sauce for dipping. Makes 6 servings

Nutrients per Serving: Calories: 25, Carbohydrate: 5g, Total Fat: <1g, Saturated Fat: <1g, Fiber: 1g

zucchini pizza bites

⅓ cup salsa

¼ pound chorizo sausage*

2 small zucchini, trimmed and cut diagonally into ¼-inch-thick slices

6 tablespoons shredded reduced-fat mozzarella cheese

Chorizo, a spicy pork sausage, is common in both Mexican and Spanish cooking. The Mexican variety (which is the kind most widely available in the U.S.) is made from raw pork while the Spanish variety is traditionally made from smoked pork. If chorizo is unavailable, substitute any variety of spicy sausage.

1. Preheat oven to 400°F. Place salsa in fine sieve and press out excess moisture; set aside to drain. Remove sausage from casing; crumble into small skillet. Cook and stir over medium heat 5 minutes or until cooked through; drain fat.

2. Place zucchini on baking sheet. Spoon 1 teaspoon drained salsa on each zucchini slice. Top with chorizo, dividing evenly among zucchini slices. Sprinkle cheese over chorizo.

3. Bake 10 minutes or until cheese is lightly browned. Serve immediately.

Makes 6 servings

Nutrients per Serving: Calories: 113, Carbohydrate: 3g, Total Fat: 8g, Saturated Fat: 3g, Fiber: 1g

TIP

Once you get used to a low GI diet, you'll appreciate the huge variety of foods that can make tasty snacks. Stock up on your favorite veggies and keep them handy and ready to eat in the refrigerator. When you crave something crunchy, you'll be able to choose zucchini, carrots, apples or radishes instead of a greasy chip.

ham & cheese "sushi" rolls

4 thin slices deli ham (about 4×4 inches)

1 package (8 ounces) cream cheese, softened

1 piece (4 inches long) seedless cucumber, quartered lengthwise (about ½ cucumber)

4 thin slices (about 4×4 inches) American or Cheddar cheese, at room temperature

1 red bell pepper, cut into thin 4-inch-long strips

1. For ham sushi, pat 1 ham slice with paper towel to remove excess moisture and place on cutting board. Spread 2 tablespoons cream cheese to edges of ham slice. Pat 1 cucumber piece with paper towel to remove excess moisture; place at edge of ham slice. Roll up tightly, pressing gently to seal. Wrap in plastic wrap; refrigerate. Repeat with remaining ham slices, cream cheese and cucumber pieces.

2. For cheese sushi, spread 2 tablespoons cream cheese to edges of 1 cheese slice. Place 2 red pepper strips at edge of cheese slice. Roll up tightly, pressing gently to seal. Wrap in plastic wrap; refrigerate. Repeat with remaining cheese slices, cream cheese and red pepper strips.

3. To serve, remove plastic wrap from ham and cheese rolls. Cut each roll into 8 (½-inch-wide) pieces.   Makes 8 servings

Nutrients per Serving: Calories: 145, Carbohydrate: 3g, Total Fat: 13g, Saturated Fat: 12g, Fiber: <1g

roasted garlic hummus

2 tablespoons Roasted Garlic (recipe follows)
1 can (about 15 ounces) chickpeas, rinsed and drained
¼ cup fresh parsley sprigs
2 tablespoons water
2 tablespoons lemon juice
½ teaspoon curry powder
⅛ teaspoon dark sesame oil
    Dash hot pepper sauce (optional)
    Pita bread wedges and fresh vegetables (optional)

1. Prepare Roasted Garlic.

2. Place chickpeas, parsley, 2 tablespoons Roasted Garlic, water, lemon juice, curry powder, sesame oil and hot pepper sauce, if desired, in food processor or blender. Cover; process until smooth.

3. Serve with pita wedges and vegetables, if desired.

Makes 6 servings

roasted garlic: Cut off top third of 1 large garlic head (not the root end) to expose cloves; discard top. Place head of garlic, trimmed end up, on 10-inch square of foil. Rub garlic generously with olive oil and sprinkle with salt. Gather foil ends together and close tightly. Roast in preheated 350°F oven 45 minutes or until cloves are golden and soft. When cool enough to handle, squeeze roasted garlic cloves from skins; discard skins.

Nutrients per Serving: Calories: 85, Carbohydrate: 15g, Total Fat: 1g, Saturated Fat: <1g, Fiber: 4g

smoked salmon roses

1 package (8 ounces) cream cheese, softened
1 tablespoon prepared horseradish
1 tablespoon minced fresh dill
1 tablespoon half-and-half
16 slices (12 to 16 ounces) smoked salmon
1 red bell pepper, cut into thin strips
Fresh dill sprigs

1. Combine cream cheese, horseradish, minced dill and half-and-half in medium bowl; beat until light and creamy.

2. Spread 1 tablespoon cream cheese mixture over each salmon slice. Roll up jelly-roll style. Cut each roll in half crosswise. Arrange salmon rolls, cut sides down, on serving dish to resemble roses. Arrange pepper strips and dill sprig in center of each rose.

Makes 16 servings (2 rolls each)

Nutrients per Serving: Calories: 80, Carbohydrate: 2g, Total Fat: 6g, Saturated Fat: 4g, Fiber: 1g

turkey, havarti & apple roll-ups

4 slices (1 ounce each) Havarti cheese
4 slices (1 ounce each) turkey
6 tablespoons Dijon-style mayonnaise
1 medium apple, cut into 8 slices

1. Place 1 slice of cheese on each slice of turkey and spread with mayonnaise.

2. Top with 2 slices of apple and roll up jelly-roll style.

Makes 4 servings

Nutrients per Serving: Calories: 156, Carbohydrate: 1g, Total Fat: 11g, Saturated Fat: 8g, Fiber: 0g

multi grain white chocolate cranberry cookies

   2 cups whole wheat flour

1 ½ cups uncooked 5-grain cereal

   1 teaspoon baking soda

   ½ teaspoon salt

   ¾ cup canola oil

   ¾ cup packed brown sugar

   ⅓ cup granulated sugar

   2 eggs

   1 tablespoon vanilla

   1 cup dried cranberries

   ½ cup white chocolate chips

1. Preheat oven to 375°F. Combine flour, cereal, baking soda and salt in medium bowl.

2. Combine oil, brown sugar, granulated sugar, eggs and vanilla in large bowl. Add flour mixture; stir to combine. Stir in cranberries and chips. Drop dough by rounded teaspoonfuls onto ungreased cookie sheets.

3. Bake 8 to 10 minutes or until golden brown but soft in center. Cool 1 minute on cookie sheets. Remove to wire racks; cool completely.

Makes 6 dozen cookies (2 cookies per serving)

Nutrients per Serving: Calories: 124, Carbohydrate: 17g, Total Fat: 6g, Saturated Fat: 1g, Fiber: 1g

glazed plum pastry

3 tablespoons sucralose-sugar blend, divided
2 tablespoons all-purpose flour
1 package (about 17 ounces) frozen puff pastry sheets, thawed
8 plums (about 2 pounds)
¼ teaspoon ground cinnamon
⅓ cup sugar-free apricot preserves

1. Preheat oven to 400°F. Line 18×12-inch baking sheet with parchment paper. Combine 2 tablespoons sugar blend and flour in medium bowl.

2. Unfold pastry sheets on prepared baking sheet. Place pastry sheets side by side so fold lines are parallel to length of baking sheet. Arrange sheets so they overlap ½ inch in center. Press center seam firmly to seal. Trim ends so pastry fits on baking sheet. Prick entire surface of pastry with fork.

3. Sprinkle sugar-flour mixture evenly over pastry to within ½ inch of edges. Bake 12 to 15 minutes until pastry is slightly puffed and golden.

4. Slice plums in half (from stem end to blossom tip); remove pits. Cut crosswise into ⅛-inch-thick slices. Arrange slices slightly overlapping in 5 rows down length of pastry. Combine remaining 1 tablespoon sugar blend and cinnamon in small bowl; sprinkle evenly over plums. Bake 15 minutes or until plums are tender and pastry is browned. Remove to wire rack.

5. Place preserves in small microwavable bowl; microwave on HIGH 30 to 40 seconds or until melted. Brush preserves over plums. Cool 10 to 15 minutes before serving. **Makes 20 servings**

Nutrients per Serving: Calories: 152, Carbohydrate: 18g, Total Fat: 8g, Saturated Fat: 2g, Fiber: 1g

strawberry & peach crisp

1 cup frozen unsweetened peach slices, thawed and cut into 1-inch pieces

1 cup sliced fresh strawberries

1 tablespoon sugar, divided

¼ cup bran cereal flakes

2 tablespoons old-fashioned oats

1 tablespoon all-purpose flour

⅛ teaspoon ground cinnamon

⅛ teaspoon salt

2 teaspoons unsalted margarine, cut into small pieces

1. Preheat oven to 325°F. Coat 1- to 1½-quart glass baking dish with nonstick cooking spray.

2. Combine peaches and strawberries in medium bowl. Sprinkle with 1 teaspoon sugar. Transfer fruit to prepared baking dish.

3. Combine cereal, oats, flour, cinnamon and salt in bowl. Stir in remaining 2 teaspoons sugar. Add margarine; stir with fork until mixture resembles coarse crumbs. Sprinkle over fruit in baking dish. Bake 20 minutes or until fruit is hot and topping is slightly browned.

Makes 4 (½-cup) servings

variation: To make a strawberry crisp, omit the peaches and use 2 cups strawberries in the recipe.

Nutrients per Serving: Calories: 80, Carbohydrate: 15g, Total Fat: 2g, Saturated Fat: <1g, Fiber: 3g

chocolate chip cherry oatmeal cookies

⅔ cup sugar

⅓ cup canola oil

¼ cup cholesterol-free egg substitute

1 teaspoon vanilla

¾ cup all-purpose flour

½ teaspoon baking soda

½ teaspoon ground cinnamon

⅛ teaspoon salt

1½ cups old-fashioned oats

¼ cup mini semisweet chocolate chips

½ cup dried cherries, raisins or cranberries

1. Preheat oven to 325°F. Spray cookie sheets with nonstick cooking spray.

2. Beat sugar, oil, egg substitute and vanilla in large bowl with electric mixer at medium speed until well blended. Add flour, baking soda, cinnamon and salt; beat until smooth. Stir in oats, chocolate chips and cherries.

3. Drop dough by rounded teaspoonfuls about 2 inches apart onto prepared cookie sheet. Bake 7 minutes (cookies will not brown). Cool cookies 2 minutes on cookie sheets. Remove to wire rack; cool completely.　　　**Makes about 4 dozen cookies (2 cookies per serving)**

Nutrients per Serving: Calories: 103, Carbohydrate: 16g, Total Fat: 4g, Saturated Fat: <1g, Fiber: 1g

apple walnut cake

¾ cup all-purpose flour

2 teaspoons baking powder

1½ teaspoons apple pie spice

¾ teaspoon salt

2½ cups chopped sliced Granny Smith apples (about 2 large apples)

¼ cup plus 2 tablespoons packed brown sugar

¾ cup sugar substitute*

4½ tablespoons margarine or butter, melted

¾ cup fat-free (skim) milk

3 eggs

1½ teaspoons vanilla

½ cup chopped walnuts

*This recipe was tested with sucralose-based sugar substitute.

1. Preheat oven to 350°F. Spray 8 -or 9-inch square baking pan with nonstick cooking spray.

2. Combine flour, baking powder, apple pie spice and salt in small bowl.

3. Place apples in prepared pan. Beat sugar, sugar substitute and margarine in medium bowl with wire whisk until blended. Whisk in milk, eggs and vanilla. Stir in flour mixture until smooth. Pour over apples. Sprinkle walnuts over batter.

4. Bake 45 to 55 minutes or until knife inserted into center comes out clean and apples are tender. Cool 10 minutes. Serve warm; refrigerate leftovers.   **Makes 9 servings**

Nutrients per Serving: Calories: 204, Carbohydrate: 23g, Total Fat: 12g, Saturated Fat: 2g, Fiber: 2g

blueberry-pear tart

1 refrigerated (9-inch) pie crust
1 medium ripe pear, peeled, cored and thinly sliced
8 ounces fresh or thawed frozen blueberries or blackberries
⅓ cup no-sugar-added raspberry fruit spread
½ teaspoon grated fresh ginger

1. Preheat oven to 450°F.

2. Spray 9-inch tart pan with nonstick cooking spray. Place pie crust in pan; press against side of pan to form ½-inch edge. Trim edges. Prick dough several times with fork. Bake 12 minutes. Remove pan to wire rack; cool completely.

3. Arrange pears on bottom of cooled crust; top with blueberries.

4. Place fruit spread in small microwavable bowl. Cover with plastic wrap; microwave on HIGH 15 seconds. Stir. If necessary, microwave additional 10 to 15 seconds or until spread is melted; stir. Add ginger; stir until blended. Let stand 30 seconds to thicken slightly. Pour mixture over fruit in crust. Refrigerate 2 hours. (Do not cover.) Cut into 8 slices.

Makes 8 servings

Nutrients per Serving: Calories: 179, Carbohydrate: 28g, Total Fat: 7g, Saturated Fat: 3g, Fiber: 2g

TIP

Who wouldn't like fruit for dessert when it's in a delicious form like this Blueberry-Pear Tart? Eating low GI doesn't mean giving up dessert, just choosing more wisely. From apples to ugli fruit there are dozens of colors and flavors of fruit to thrill your taste buds.

grapefruit sorbet

1 large pink grapefruit
½ cup apple juice
1 ½ tablespoons sugar

1. Peel grapefruit; remove white pith. Cut into segments over bowl to catch juices, removing membranes between segments. Combine grapefruit, grapefruit juice, apple juice and sugar in food processor or blender; purée until smooth.

2. Process grapefruit mixture in ice cream machine according to manufacturer's directions. Serve immediately.

Makes 1 ⅓ cups (4 servings)

Nutrients per Serving: Calories: 59, Carbohydrate: 15g, Total Fat: 0g, Saturated Fat: 0g, Fiber: 1g

peaches with raspberry sauce

1 cup raspberries
½ cup water
¼ cup sugar substitute
6 peach halves
⅓ cup vanilla fat-free yogurt

1. Combine raspberries, water and sugar substitute in small saucepan; bring to a boil over medium-high heat, stirring frequently. Boil 1 minute. Transfer to food processor or blender; process until smooth. Set aside 15 minutes to cool.

2. Drizzle ¼ cup raspberry sauce onto each of 6 serving dishes. Place one peach half on each dish. Spoon about 2½ teaspoons yogurt over each peach half.

Makes 6 servings

Nutrients per Serving: Calories: 41, Carbohydrate: 10g, Total Fat: 0g, Saturated Fat: 0g, Fiber: 2g

chewy mocha brownie cookies

1 cup all-purpose flour
¼ teaspoon baking soda
¼ cup stick margarine
⅔ cup granulated sugar
⅓ cup unsweetened cocoa powder
¼ cup firmly packed brown sugar
1½ teaspoons instant coffee granules
¼ cup reduced-fat buttermilk
1 teaspoon vanilla
2 tablespoons powdered sugar

1. Combine flour and baking soda in small bowl. Melt margarine in medium saucepan; remove from heat. Stir in granulated sugar, cocoa, brown sugar and coffee granules. Add buttermilk and vanilla; mix well. Stir in flour mixture just until combined. Transfer dough to small bowl. Cover and refrigerate 1 hour. (Dough will be stiff.)

2. Preheat oven to 350°F. Lightly spray cookie sheets with nonstick cooking spray or line with parchment paper. Drop dough by rounded teaspoonfuls onto prepared cookie sheets.

3. Bake 10 to 11 minutes or until edges are firm. Cool on cookie sheets 2 minutes. Remove to wire rack; cool completely.

4. Sprinkle with powdered sugar just before serving.

Makes 2 dozen cookies (2 cookies per serving)

Nutrients per Serving: Calories: 142, Carbohydrate: 26g, Total Fat: 4g, Saturated Fat: 1g, Fiber: 1g

chocolate mousse minis

1 envelope unflavored gelatin

¼ cup water

¾ cup reduced-fat evaporated milk

1 egg yolk

⅓ cup unsweetened cocoa powder

⅓ cup semisweet chocolate chips

½ teaspoon vanilla

½ cup sugar substitute*

¾ cup plus 6 tablespoons reduced-fat whipped topping, divided

3 chocolate wafer cookies, crumbled

*This recipe was tested with sucralose-based sugar substitute.

1. Sprinkle gelatin over water in medium saucepan. Let stand about 2 minutes or until gelatin softens. Whisk in evaporated milk, egg yolk and cocoa powder. Bring to a low simmer over medium heat; cook and stir 2 minutes or until mixture is smooth and slightly thickened.

2. Remove from heat; whisk in chocolate chips, vanilla and sugar substitute until smooth. Transfer to medium bowl; let cool to room temperature, stirring every 5 minutes.

3. Fold in ¾ cup whipped topping until smooth. Spoon about ¼ cup mousse into 6 (4-ounce) dessert glasses. Cover and refrigerate 1 hour.

4. To serve, top each glass with 1 tablespoon whipped topping and 1½ teaspoons cookie crumbs. **Makes 6 servings**

Nutrients per Serving: Calories: 138, Carbohydrate: 19g, Total Fat: 7g, Saturated Fat: 3g, Fiber: 2g

panna cotta with mango sauce

1 ½ teaspoons unflavored gelatin

3 tablespoons cold water

¾ cup fat-free half-and-half

¼ cup sugar

1 teaspoon grated lemon peel

¾ cup reduced-fat buttermilk

¾ cup fresh or frozen mango chunks

2 teaspoons lemon juice

2 teaspoons sugar

1. Sprinkle gelatin over water in small heavy saucepan. Let stand about 2 minutes or until gelatin softens. Stir in half-and-half, sugar and lemon peel; cook and stir over low heat until gelatin is dissolved. *Do not boil.* Remove from heat; strain into medium bowl. Stir in buttermilk. Cool 20 minutes, stirring occasionally.

2. Divide mixture among 4 (6-ounce) custard cups or ramekins. Cover with plastic wrap; refrigerate at least 4 hours or until set.

3. Meanwhile, blend mango, lemon juice and sugar in blender or food processor until smooth; strain into small bowl. Refrigerate until ready to serve.

4. Using thin sharp knife, cut around inside edge of each cup to loosen. Dip bottom of 1 cup into bowl of very warm water about 5 seconds. Place dessert plate upside down over cup and invert, gently lifting off cup to allow panna cotta to settle onto plate. Repeat with remaining panna cottas. Serve with mango sauce. **Makes 4 servings**

Nutrients per Serving: Calories: 131, Carbohydrate: 27g, Total Fat: <1g, Saturated Fat: <1g, Fiber: 1g

METRIC CONVERSION CHART

VOLUME MEASUREMENTS (dry)

1/8 teaspoon = 0.5 mL
1/4 teaspoon = 1 mL
1/2 teaspoon = 2 mL
3/4 teaspoon = 4 mL
1 teaspoon = 5 mL
1 tablespoon = 15 mL
2 tablespoons = 30 mL
1/4 cup = 60 mL
1/3 cup = 75 mL
1/2 cup = 125 mL
2/3 cup = 150 mL
3/4 cup = 175 mL
1 cup = 250 mL
2 cups = 1 pint = 500 mL
3 cups = 750 mL
4 cups = 1 quart = 1 L

VOLUME MEASUREMENTS (fluid)

1 fluid ounce (2 tablespoons) = 30 mL
4 fluid ounces (1/2 cup) = 125 mL
8 fluid ounces (1 cup) = 250 mL
12 fluid ounces (1 1/2 cups) = 375 mL
16 fluid ounces (2 cups) = 500 mL

WEIGHTS (mass)

1/2 ounce = 15 g
1 ounce = 30 g
3 ounces = 90 g
4 ounces = 120 g
8 ounces = 225 g
10 ounces = 285 g
12 ounces = 360 g
16 ounces = 1 pound = 450 g

DIMENSIONS

1/16 inch = 2 mm
1/8 inch = 3 mm
1/4 inch = 6 mm
1/2 inch = 1.5 cm
3/4 inch = 2 cm
1 inch = 2.5 cm

OVEN TEMPERATURES

250°F = 120°C
275°F = 140°C
300°F = 150°C
325°F = 160°C
350°F = 180°C
375°F = 190°C
400°F = 200°C
425°F = 220°C
450°F = 230°C

BAKING PAN SIZES

Utensil	Size in Inches/Quarts	Metric Volume	Size in Centimeters
Baking or Cake Pan (square or rectangular)	8×8×2	2 L	20×20×5
	9×9×2	2.5 L	23×23×5
	12×8×2	3 L	30×20×5
	13×9×2	3.5 L	33×23×5
Loaf Pan	8×4×3	1.5 L	20×10×7
	9×5×3	2 L	23×13×7
Round Layer Cake Pan	8×1½	1.2 L	20×4
	9×1½	1.5 L	23×4
Pie Plate	8×1¼	750 mL	20×3
	9×1¼	1 L	23×3
Baking Dish or Casserole	1 quart	1 L	—
	1½ quart	1.5 L	—
	2 quart	2 L	—